Confessions of a Depressed Christian

How a Pastor Survived Depression

and How You Can Too

Jason R. McNaughten

About the Author

Jason is married to his lovely wife Lori and has two daughters. He has pastored churches in Missouri and Louisiana and is currently the pastor of First Baptist Church, New Roads, LA. He received his Master of Divinity from Midwestern Baptist Theological Seminary and his Doctorate of Ministry from New Orleans Baptist Theological Seminary. Jason is an avid runner and has participated in numerous 5k's and marathons.

Table of Contents

Acknowledgements

I would not have written this book without the support and encouragement of Lori, my wife. I am also appreciative of friends and family who have encouraged me to write, especially Carla Martin. Also, I acknowledge my parents. My father is with the Lord, but has greatly influenced my life. My mother continues to be a source of great joy and love. Thanks also to Beverly Stuart, my ministry assistant, who was part of the editing process.

Introduction

Depression can be shameful. In *The Scarlet Letter,* Hester Prynne is caught in an adulterous affair. She must wear a scarlet "A" on her dress. The "A" is a symbol of shame for her sin. I have never committed adultery, but I have struggled with depression. At times I have felt like an outcast, as if I was wearing a "D" for depression, rather than an "A" for adultery. I have learned that I have no reason to be ashamed of my depression. You have no reason to be ashamed either. If you are a Christian, you especially have no reason to live in shame. You can be a solid, Bible-believing, Christ-loving Christian and still struggle with depression.

I am a Christian who has struggled with depression. I also have the unique perspective of being a pastor who has struggled with depression. I still wrestle with depression at times, but I had an especially dark time in my life. The following recounts my dark days of depression and how I survived, and still survive today. **I confess, "I was hesitant to write this book."** Making private struggles public is not something I am comfortable doing. I have decided to share my struggle in spite of my misgivings. It has resulted in the book you now have in your possession. Perhaps you are dealing with depression, or have a loved one who is depressed. Maybe you are just curious about Christianity and depression. It is my hope and prayer that this book will be of great encouragement to you.

Writing this book was not as easy as anticipated. It is far more real and personal than planned. I hope you can relate to and appreciate my transparency. Writing my story has been therapeutic to my own life and soul. Perhaps it would benefit you to write your own story. Above all, I have written this to bring glory and honor to Christ. My story is not as important as THE STORY, the story of God's love through Jesus Christ. To Him be glory and honor. I have not written this book from the perspective of a professional counselor, psychiatrist, or medical doctor. My perspective is a personal and spiritual one. I am a follower of Christ and a pastor of a local church. These are the confessions of a depressed Christian.

Chapter 1

MY CONFESSION

I ran 31 miles by accident. I was running a marathon, which is 26.2 miles. I missed the left turn at mile 21. It was not my first marathon. I am a seasoned veteran that made a rookie mistake. I didn't know how to get back on course. No one else knew either.

I had two choices. I could call for a race official to pick me up, which would result in a disqualification, or I could plod along and keep running. I kept running and eventually crossed the finish line. Instead of completing the marathon in less than four hours, I ran for five hours. I was disgusted when I finally finished. Now I am glad I missed the turn. I had never run more than 26.2 miles before the incident. Now I know I can run 31 miles. I suppose I could run 41 miles if need be.

Life is like running. It has its peaks and valleys, victories and defeats. How you respond makes all the difference. If life is like running, depression is an ultra-marathon. It is long and grueling. It seems like a missed turn that morphs into a miserable journey. You seem lost and don't know where the finish line is. No one can seemingly point you in the right direction either. You have two choices. You can give up, or plod along and keep going. Depression has been a real part of my life and ministry. At times I wanted to give up, but I have decided to plod along and keep going. This book is a peek into my own personal journey of depression, my missed turn if you will.

I confess, "I am a Christian who has struggled with depression." I admit it. It is now a matter of public record. I am not confessing a horrific sin. I have committed no serious crime. It sounds silly, but struggling with depression is not an easy confession to make. I am not ashamed of my depression, but depression does carry a certain stigma with it. To some, depression is a plague of shame, a scarlet letter that stains the soul and reputation. It is hard enough to admit being depressed. To complicate matters, I am a Christian who has struggled with depression. A depressed Christian sounds like an oxymoron. Christianity and depression are as compatible as peanut butter and gunpowder or snow storms and the Caribbean.

Christians are to be a people of joy. James wrote, in **James 1:2**, "Consider it all joy, my brethren, when you encounter various trials." No matter what we face, and no matter how depressing life gets, we are to count it all joy. It does not mean we have to be excited about a certain trial or tribulation. It does mean we can respond to life's challenges and burdens with a joyful attitude. Consider the apostle Paul, a man of heroic faith. Paul had numerous trials and tribulations. He was beaten, thrown into prison, stoned, and shipwrecked. Read about the struggles and trials of Paul when you are having a crummy day. It will change your perspective. He maintained an attitude of joy in the midst of it all.

Paul wrote, in **Philippians 4:4,** "Rejoice in the Lord always, again I will say rejoice." A few verses later he proclaims he is content whether he has everything or nothing. He reveals the secret in **Philippians 4:13**, "I can do all things through Him (Christ) who strengthens me." Paul practiced what he preached. For example, Acts 16 records the imprisonment of both Paul and Silas. They are not in prison for robbing a bank or cheating the government. They are chained for preaching the Gospel. It would be easy to respond with discouragement and depression. How do they respond? They sing with joy! Depression is like being in prison. You are bound by the chains of pain and anxiety. It is hard to rejoice and count it all joy like Paul and Silas did.

Some well-intentioned Christians think depression is either a sin or a lack of faith in God. But being depressed is not a sin, nor is it always the result of a sin. One may say, for instance, "If Paul can sing with joy in prison, why should any Christian be depressed?" Someone else might reason, "If you really believe the Bible, trust Christ, and know God is in control, how could you ever be depressed? Just pray harder and read the Bible. Love Jesus and the depression will be lifted."

Maybe you have been told that and feel like a spiritual loser. You pray, read the Bible, attend church, and still are depressed. Praying, reading the Bible, and loving Jesus are important; yet, Christians get depressed. In 2011, the Center for Disease Control revealed that at least 1 in 10 Americans struggle with depression. If your church averages 100 in attendance, for instance, odds are that at least ten of them deal with depression. Chances are someone in your family struggles as well.

Depression is not an indicator of being a spiritual loser. Depression is not a sign of being weak either. Strong, successful people get depressed. Abraham Lincoln, the 16th President of the United States, struggled with depression. Winton Churchill, the former Prime Minister of the United Kingdom, wrestled with depression too. Churchill referred to depression as his "black dog." Good and godly leaders deal with depression. Martin Luther, whom God used to spark the Protestant Reformation, had fits of depression. Charles Spurgeon is known as the Prince of Preachers. Spurgeon preached to thousands, wrote an abundance of books, and was used mightily of God. He had dark times of depression. Spurgeon noted:

> Fits of depression come over the most of us. Cheerful as we may be, we must at intervals be cast down. The strong are not always vigorous, the wise not always ready, the brave not always courageous, and the joyous not always happy…This depression comes over me whenever the Lord is preparing a larger blessing for my ministry. The cloud is black before it breaks and overshadows before it yields its deluge of mercy. Depression has now become to me as a prophet in rough

clothing, a John the Baptist heralding the nearer coming of my Lord's richer benison (blessings). So have far better men found it. The scouring of the vessel has fitted it for the Master's use.[1]

You are not a second-class citizen if you deal with depression. You are not on the bottom of the Christian food chain either. I have to remind myself of that reality, especially when I am depressed. It is not easy being a depressed Christian. It is certainly not easy being a depressed pastor. While burdened with depression, I have had to preach, pray, visit the sick, and leap tall buildings in a single bound. People often have unrealistic expectations of pastors. Some even see pastors as beyond human. Pastors are people too. We have bad days, headaches, and even dark times of depression. If I were Superman, depression would be my kryptonite.

> *Depression is not an indicator of being a spiritual loser.*

I carried the shame of being a depressed Christian for a while. I also carried the shame of being a depressed pastor. My wife knew about it of course, but not my church or immediate family. God convicted me of my silence. How can I help others with depression if I remain silent about my own depression? Paul wrote, in **2 Corinthians 1:4**, that God "comforts us in all our affliction so that we will be able to comfort those who are in any affliction with the comfort with which we ourselves are comforted by God." God has indeed comforted me in times of depression. He wants to use me to comfort others who are depressed.

Perhaps you are struggling, or have struggled, with depression. Perhaps God wants to use you to encourage others. Maybe you have a family member who is depressed. Perhaps you are just curious about a pastor and his depression. I still struggle with depression at times, but I had an especially dark time in my life. The following recounts my dark days of depression and how I survived, and still survive today.

Questions for reflection:

1. Are you keeping your depression a secret?

2. Do you feel guilty and less of a Christian for being depressed?

3 Are you surprised by the depression of Luther,
  Spurgeon, Lincoln, and Churchill?

Notes:

Chapter 2

MY JOURNEY INTO DEPRESSION

The National Guard went on a search and rescue for my dog. Houdini, my Jack Russell Terrier, was a fuzz ball of energy. His groomer once remarked, "What do you feed him, gun powder!" The name Houdini is no coincidence. Like the great magician, he always found a way of escaping. My in-laws were in town spoiling the grandkids, so my wife and I decided to watch a movie. The plans were interrupted with a frantic phone call. Houdini had escaped. My mother-in-law and my oldest daughter searched the area. The neighbors helped too. A National Guard Armory is located less than a mile from my house. A few guardsmen took notice and sent out two or three search teams. Houdini was eventually cornered and captured.

Houdini has since passed away. He was like another member of my family. Though he loved our family, Houdini was a natural hunter. So he yearned to escape our backyard in hot pursuit of a squirrel, cat, or dog. Like Houdini, we want to be free and rejoice in God's good creation. Depression, at times, seems like you're fenced in. For me, I had times where I yearned to be free and live with joy. I wanted to escape the backyard of my depression. Most people get down and have brief periods of depression and discouragement. My depression far exceeded the Monday blues. The days and weeks turned into months and years.

I was not just sad. **I confess, "Depression crippled my whole life at times."** I think all of us have dark places in our hearts. Some of us are more prone to linger in the darkness. I was in an exceedingly dark place at one particular point in my life. Depression crippled me physically, emotionally, mentally, and spiritually. My depression, like a heavy fog, lingered for eight years. My depression was not for eight consecutive years. It stayed two years and drifted away, only to resurface a few years later. The pattern repeated itself. It was a vicious cycle with no end in sight.

I have been free from serious depression for several years now. I do have brief periods of depression, but they do not linger long. If I ever do fall back into a long-term depression, I am better equipped to respond in a way that promotes health and healing. Depression can be a result of several factors. A few reasons are emotional pain and loss, negative thinking, low self-esteem, and inward anger. Depression has also been linked with physical factors like genetics, diet, lifestyle, and seasonal changes. I believe my prolonged period of depression was a result of three main factors:

---

3 Causes of My Depression

---

1. CHANGE

My descent into depression began while attending seminary. I loved seminary. I enjoyed studying Theology, Greek, and Church History. I made good friends who loved and served the Lord. My marriage was healthy and vibrant. In the midst of all the good things, something was not right. The check engine light of my soul came on. **I confess, "I felt sad all the time."** I was emotional and irritable. I had no motivation or energy. I dreaded getting out of bed. My soul was a barren desert. I did the only thing I knew to do at the time; I talked to a seminary professor. He is a professional counselor who has dealt with his own bouts of depression. He referred me to a friend of his, another Christian counselor. Getting counseling gave me insight into my battle with depression. It was my first step out of the darkness.

While I cherished studying at seminary and being in the ministry, it was a drastic change to my life. My mom and dad ran a small, yet successful printing business. I grew up planning to take over the family business. My wife and I got married and bought a home close to family. I then graduated from college with a business degree. My father was preparing to retire, and I was going to step in and take the lead. The course of my life was set, or so I thought. Everything changed in 1999, when I surrendered to vocational ministry.

When I began to sense God calling me to vocational ministry, I pulled a Jonah and ran. Thankfully, there was no large fish to swallow me! I delayed surrendering to God because being a pastor is a serious and life-long commitment. Not only that, my life was already settled. My calling, or so I thought, was to carry on the family business. I also ran from God's calling because I was naturally shy and reserved. Being a public speaker and public figure was not on my wish list. I could relate well to Moses who said, in **Exodus 4:10**, "Please, Lord, I have never been eloquent, neither recently nor in time past, since You have spoken to Your servant; for I am slow of speech and slow of tongue." I finally obeyed God and surrendered to the ministry.

My wife and I sold our house, packed up everything, and moved to Kansas City, Missouri for me to attend Midwestern Baptist Theological Seminary.

I entered my first bout of deep depression while at seminary. I believe change was a contributing factor. My life radically changed in the course of a few years. Being a pastor was not in the plans. Moving wasn't either. My wife and I left all our family and moved 500 miles away. I went from being in business to being in the ministry. More changes were yet to come.

Change is part of life. Change, even good change, can lead to stress, weariness, and depression. A great truth to remember is that God does not change. Malachi writes, in **Malachi 3:6**, "For I, the LORD, do not change." Regardless of what change you may be facing, God never changes! You can always count on Him.

2. DISAPPOINTMENT

While I was struggling with change, my wife and I desperately wanted children. We were trying to start a family long before I entered the ministry. We were the first of our friends to get married and the last to be parents. When all of our friends had children we publicly celebrated and secretly mourned. Our home and hearts were empty. The doctor said everything looked okay after several tests and procedures. The green light was given to start a family. Nothing happened. Each failed pregnancy test was a kick in the gut. We were on an emotional roller coaster for eleven years. It was sheer agony.

I confess, "My wife and I were disappointed and devastated." Infertility was a constant thorn in our flesh. Like the apostle Paul we prayed numerous times for God to remove it, but God had to remind us, "My grace is sufficient." So far, infertility has been the worst trial of my life. However, it was a source of an even greater blessing. We began the adoption process after about nine years of infertility. Two years later we adopted our first daughter.

Looking back we would not change a thing. We knew God was in control of the process, and our daughter was a confirmation of that reality. That was not the end of God's blessings. We got the surprise of a lifetime when our oldest daughter was seven. A friend called my wife and asked if we were interested in adopting again. We prayed about it and a week later brought home the second addition to our family, another precious baby girl. God has far exceeded our hopes and dreams.

> *A great truth to remember is that God does not change.*

Infertility was not the only source of disappointment. I began my first full time pastorate right after graduating from seminary. It was a good church, and the people loved my wife and me. The church saw considerable growth. Things were going well, yet I fell back into the rut of depression. I believe change was still a contributing factor. I was still getting used to the idea of being a pastor, as well as being away from home. The reality of ministry hit too. Being a pastor for the first time was eye-opening. It is no easy task.

It is one thing to study at seminary to become a pastor, it is quite another thing to be a pastor. God called me to the task, but I was learning what the call really entailed. Being a pastor involved more than teaching the Bible, visiting nice folks, and attending pot-luck suppers. I rubbed shoulders with death, disappointment, and heartache. I stood in a hospital room while they pulled the ventilator on someone, thus leading to her death. I ministered to a family whose little boy drowned. I dealt with people telling me I was "too young to be a pastor." I thought, "What am I supposed to do until I am the right age? What age is that?" On a lighter note, a woman in the church called me to babysit her dog. I thought, "I went to seminary for this? I am not the pope of pooches!"

While I love being a pastor, it lends itself to disappointment. People disappoint you. You are exposed to the dark and dirty sides of their lives. Situations at church can be disappointing as well. Here is as entry from my journal that gives a picture into my soul: *November 16, 2005*, "Life seems to be a blur, a great mystery. As per God, I seem to know Him no longer. Things used to be so certain and straightforward. I would work, enjoy life, spend time with family and friends, and then enjoy an hour or so with my Lord. But, now life is no longer compartmentalized as it once was. I have no family here, apart from Lori, nor do I have any friends here. I have a job that seemingly separates me from everything else. A pastor is not just what I do; it is who I am. As a result, my life has been greatly shaken and changed and turned about." I was learning to be a pastor and how to deal with the struggles and pain that followed.

3. LOSS

I enjoyed my first pastorate. I will always cherish those first years of ministry. Lifelong friendships were established. Soon after my oldest daughter's adoption another church called me as their pastor. It was a church in Louisiana, my home state. I accepted the call and moved back home, only one hour away from family. My wife was able to stay home as a fulltime mother too. My second pastorate was quite contrary to my first. Instead of growth, it shrunk. Instead of peace and unity, conflict thrived. Feelings were hurt and relationships were damaged. It was a hard pill to swallow. My wife and I had never experienced anything like this before.

I confess, "I felt like a failure." I literally felt like someone, or something had died. I still hurt thinking about what happened. I felt God wanted me to stay after the storm, so I stayed at the church four more years. I learned a lot about ministry and myself during that time. Though it was a difficult experience, the people at the church were and still are a great blessing to my life. Someone observed, "Life is like photography. We develop from the negatives." The Lord was using this pastorate to make me the leader and pastor I needed to be. Hard times, even times of loss, make us more like Christ. Paul wrote, in **Romans 5:3-4**, "And not only this, but we also exalt in our tribulations, knowing that tribulation brings about perseverance; and perseverance, proven character; and proven character, hope."

The church was not my only source of loss at the time. My father died of cancer. He was the epitome of health, until cancer struck. My journal entry reveals my struggles with his sickness. *May 17, 2008*, "The last few days have been hard to describe. Dad has been in the hospital sick. More than that, the prognosis is leaning towards cancer. He has a mass on his lungs and probably in his throat as well. My dad has been the epitome of health my entire life. It seems absurd, but the last few days I have been contemplating dad's funeral. It is a strange thought because he is still alive. But, perhaps it is my way of dealing with the loss and thinking of how his life has impacted mine."

My fear came true. He passed away two months later. It was a shock to my family. My father was not just my dad; he was my hero and best friend. He is still my hero and always will be. His death was a great loss. While grieving the loss of my dad, I was still grieving the events at church. In the book of Job, Job lost everything in one fell swoop. He still praised God. I had not lost everything, but it seemed like it. I was searching for a way to praise God.

Maybe you are in a time of loss. You feel like a failure. A loved one has died. Something didn't turn out as you had imagined. Grieve the loss. Cry. Be honest about your emotions. It is understood that grief has five stages: Denial, Anger, Bargaining, Depression, and Acceptance. What stage of grief are you in? Are you properly grieving your losses? Loss, disappointment, and change were not the only issues that led to my depression, but they were certainly the major contributors.

Questions for reflection:

1. What changes have you experienced over the past year?

2. Could disappointment be a factor in your depression?

3. Have you properly grieved your losses?

Notes:

Chapter 3

THE PAIN OF DEPRESSION

"Toto, I have a feeling we're not in Kansas anymore." Judy Garland coined those famous words in the classic film *The Wizard of Oz*. It is one of my oldest daughter's favorite movies. It is also a picture of my depression. A violent tornado sweeps Dorothy away. She lands in Oz, a land far away from home. It is a strange, yet fascinating world of witches, flying monkeys, and munchkins. It seems all a dream. Despite the wonder of Oz, Dorothy yearns to be home, to go back to life as it once was. All she has to do is click her ruby slippers and say, "There's no place like home. There's no place like home. There's no place like home." Dorothy goes back to Kansas. All is well, and she lives happily ever after.

What does *The Wizard of Oz* have to do with my depression? The dark clouds of depression swept me away from life as I knew it. I didn't wind up in Oz, but I was in a strange, yet fascinating world, the Land of Depression. Instead of witches, flying monkeys, and the yellow brick road, it was full of pain and sorrow. Life seemed like a dream, not a good dream mind you. If only I could click my shoes three times and repeat, "There's no place like home." If only I could get out of the Land of Depression and back to the way life once was.

I confess, "I was in a lot of pain." The pain was not primarily physical; it was emotional and mental. In some ways depression is more troubling than physical pain. People understand physical pain. You break an arm and people see your cast and understand, to some degree, what you are going through. You can visit a doctor without fear and shame. You can tell your friends and family about your experience. They understand and even feel sorry for you. Not so with depression. Most people do not understand the pain of depression. Depression is not as visible as a broken arm. It is not treated as easily either. You cannot put a cast or bandage on depression. It doesn't heal in a matter of weeks or days. It is embarrassing to go and see a doctor, especially for men. Most people will not even know you are depressed.

When, and if you tell your family members and friends about your depression, they may not understand. Some may even mock your pain or question your sanity. There are numerous types of depression. Many who are depressed readily identify with Major Depressive Disorder, better known as clinical depression. The term "clinical depression" may bring to mind white coats, electroshock therapy, or being committed to an insane asylum. It doesn't mean you are crazy, unstable, or incompetent. It simply means you have "five (or more) of the following symptoms during the same 2-week period... At least one of the symptoms is either (1) depressed mood or (2) loss of interest or pleasure."[2]

□ Depressed mood most of the day, nearly every day

□ Loss of interest or pleasure in most activities

□ Significant weight loss or gain

□ Sleeping too much or not enough

□ Slowed thinking or movement that others can see

□ Fatigue or low energy nearly every day

□ Feelings of worthlessness or inappropriate guilt

□ Loss of concentration or indecisiveness

□ Recurring thoughts of death or suicide

Perhaps you can identify with one or more of the symptoms. Perhaps it describes your exact struggle. Maybe your depression has taken on a different form. Not everyone with depression will fit the mold. Men can especially differ from the classic signs. Depression in men tends to surface more as anger than sadness.[3] Depression is often associated with anxiety as well. For some, depression entails serious medical conditions such as bipolar disorder. Seek a professional for diagnosis if you think you are depressed.

Maybe you deal with clinical depression. You have seen a medical doctor and perhaps a counselor of some type. Maybe you have short seasons of darkness and sorrow. Maybe you are not sure what you have. You just know you are depressed and cannot seem to shake it. William Styron, in *Darkness Visible: a Memoir of Madness,* wrote:

In depression the faith in deliverance, in ultimate restoration, is absent. The pain is unrelenting, and what makes the condition intolerable is the foreknowledge that no remedy will come—not in a day, an hour, a month, or a minute. If there is mild relief, one knows that it is only temporary; more pain will follow. It is hopelessness even more than pain that crushes the soul. So the decision-making of daily life involves not, as in normal affairs, shifting from one annoying situation to another less annoying—or from discomfort to relative comfort, or from boredom to activity—but moving from pain to pain.

I can certainly connect with Styron's perspective. I lost the pleasure of everyday life. Though I had reasons to rejoice and celebrate, I felt numb to it all. I was miserable even while on vacation or spending quality moments with my wife. I felt worthless and sad. I lacked energy. The hardest part of my day was just getting out of the bed. I remember several times, while in my office studying, I would lay my head on my desk and zone out. I had no energy or desire. I still had hope in God, but I lost hope in life.

I confess, "Everything seemed hopeless and pointless." I am a pastor, so I am supposed to be a source of hope and joy. I had neither. Nothing seemed to matter. I was irritable too. I felt like a total failure because of my depression. I thought something was wrong with me, that I was less than human. By not disclosing my depression to my family and church family, I felt like I was living a lie. I felt ashamed and defeated. My being depressed also took a toll on my wife. I felt I had let her down.

> *Despite all of its drawbacks, depression became comfortable.*

Here is an entry from my journal. *July 28, 2008*, "In Psalm 6, David is expressing grief and sorrow. His enemies overwhelm him. David fears for his very life. At night he cries and saturates his bed with tears. By day his eyes waste away with grief. He is seeking vengeance upon his enemies and comfort from the Lord. Some things in my life seemingly relate to David's predicament. I think of the years Lori and I struggled with infertility. Some days my soul was in great agony, and I was overwhelmed with sorrow. The caverns of depression are another such episode. Recently, the conflict at church has caused much sorrow and pain. Lastly, my dad's passing is fresh upon me. My soul and bones are dismayed. I am weary with tears and burdened with sadness. In the tough times God is there. The Lord is gracious to hear my prayers and take heed to my sad condition. Lord, deliver me today and give me strength to endure."

My depression was a vicious cycle. I was tired because I was irritable. I became irritable because I was tired. I didn't enjoy life because I was depressed. I became more depressed because I didn't enjoy life. I felt depressed because I felt worthless. Because I felt worthless I lacked energy and motivation.

Depression is a vicious cycle. Have you ever had a washing machine get unbalanced? The machine gets wobbly and noisy. Depression is an unbalanced spin cycle. Everything is wobbly and off kilter. I never thought I would recover. My soul was in constant winter. Spring seemed like an unattainable reality. Another depression survivor observed, "Depression lies to us that we'll never get better. In the midst of the storm we look both back and ahead and see nothing but the high winds, fog, and darkness. As we look back we think, 'I've been like this so long that I can't remember what it felt like to feel good.'"[4]

I confess, "I forgot what it was like to be happy." I believed I was not worthy of anything but depression. Depression became like a pair of jeans. Have you ever had a favorite pair of old jeans? They are torn and tattered from repeated use. The jeans may be faded or ripped. You need to throw them away, but you hesitate. Why? You feel at home in the jeans, regardless of their flaws.

Depression became an old pair of jeans to me. Despite all of its drawbacks, depression became comfortable. It was all I had known. It became a way for me to cope with the pain and struggles of life. Depression became my friend. It was a painful friendship indeed.

It may seem strange for a Christian to be depressed. It is even stranger to hear about a pastor being depressed. Depression in the ministry is common. The Shaeffer Institute reveals approximately 70% of pastors battle with depression.[5] Why are so many pastors depressed? **I confess, "Being a minister is not always easy."** Pastors constantly feel inadequate. They are on call 24/7. They struggle with loneliness, problems in the church, and unrealistic demands. Pastors deal with the burdens of their life, but also the lives of those whom they serve. In the course of one week a pastor may face a crisis in the church, counsel a troubled married couple, and visit someone dying in the hospital. Not only that, a pastor is seemingly given prayer requests on a daily basis. All the while, he has his own problems and life events to deal with.

Pastors are flawed and deal with temptation and sin like everyone else. They are asked questions they cannot always answer and presented with problems they cannot fix. Many pastors either burn out or abandon ship. Please don't get the wrong impression. It is a blessing to be a pastor. Nevertheless, odds are your pastor has struggled with depression. Pray for your pastor and the leadership of your church. Let this be an encouragement to you. If pastors battle with depression, it is no surprise that other Christians do too. You are not alone in the struggle.

Questions for reflection:

1. What pain are you feeling because of depression?

2. Do you feel like you deserve your depression? Why?

3. Do you remember what it was like to be truly happy?

4. Do you know a godly person who has struggled with depression?

Notes:

Jason R. McNaughten

Chapter 4

THE BIBLE AND DEPRESSION

What is your favorite comfort food? Maybe it is macaroni and cheese or biscuits and gravy. Perhaps pizza or French fries do the trick. What about fried chicken or grilled cheese sandwiches? I love all the above, but my favorite is peanut butter and jelly sandwiches. I remember as a kid not always wanting what my mother cooked. When that happened I usually opted for a peanut butter and jelly sandwich, with a tall glass of milk. The same is still true today. Some days all I want is that comforting taste of peanut butter and jelly. It is not ideal to run to food for comfort; however, certain foods just make us feel at ease and okay.

Jesus said, in **Matthew 4:4**, "It is written 'Man shall not live on bread alone, but on every word that proceeds out of the mouth of God.'" I suppose He also meant man should not live on peanut butter and jelly alone. The supernatural, specifically God's word, is more important than the natural, bread. This is true especially in times of darkness. We should read the Bible on a daily basis regardless of our circumstances. We should especially turn to it when discouraged and depressed. The Bible is often viewed as broccoli or cauliflower. We know it is good for us, but we don't pay attention to its words. The Bible is our soul food, a source of supernatural comfort. Unlike fried chicken or pizza, it is always good for you.

The Bible is sometimes avoided because people have wrong ideas about depression. It is sometimes seen as a lack of faith. The Bible tells us to have joy. Therefore, it is reasoned, anything less than joy offends God and is sin. God does want us to be joyful, but we live in a fallen and sinful world. Humanity has its real struggles, even faithful followers of God struggle. Even the heroes of the Bible had bad days. Moses murdered someone. Noah got drunk and naked. Abraham lied about his marriage to Sarah. David committed adultery with Bathsheba. The super saints of the Bible got frustrated, dealt with anger, and even struggled with depression. The pages of the Bible are stained with tears and sorrow.

Examples of Depression in the Bible

JEREMIAH

Jeremiah was a great prophet of God. He was a man of boldness and faithfulness. He spoke the truth when no one else would. Yet, he is known as the weeping prophet. Have you ever heard of the book of Lamentations? Jeremiah is lamenting, or mourning, over the fall of Jerusalem. Jeremiah, in **Jeremiah 9:1**, reveals his sorrow, "Oh that my head were waters and my eyes a fountain of tears, that I might weep day and night for the slain of the daughter of my people!"

Consider Jeremiah's words in **Jeremiah 4:19**, "My soul, my soul! I am in anguish! Oh my heart! My heart is pounding in me; I cannot keep silent, because you have heard, O my soul, the sound of the trumpet, the alarm of war." Your town may not be in destruction, yet your world may seem to be. If Jeremiah had such emotions, why should we be exempt?

> *The pages of the Bible are stained with tears and sorrow.*

NAOMI

Naomi, whose story is found in the book of Ruth, had a terrible season of loss. Her husband and two sons die in a famine. She is in such sorrow and despair she changes her name from Naomi; which means "pleasant," to Mara, which means, "bitter." The name of someone in Biblical times meant far more than just what someone was called. One's name represented the very character and essence of the person. Naomi was so miserable her entire identity was characterized by bitterness. She changed her name to reflect that reality. Like Naomi, a depressed person's whole outlook and character can change from pleasantness to bitterness.

PSALM 42

The psalmist yearns to be back in the temple. He cries out, in **Psalm 42:2-5**:

My soul thirsts for God, for the living God; when shall I appear before God? My tears have been my food day and night, while they say to me all day long, "Where is your God?" These things I remember and I pour out my soul within me. For I used to go along with the throng and lead them in the procession to the house of God, with the voice of joy and thanksgiving, a multitude keeping festival. Why are you in despair, O my soul? And why have you become disturbed within me? Hope in God, for I shall again praise Him for the help of His presence.

Like the psalmist, the soul of the depressed may feel disturbed, agitated, and in despair.

ELIJAH

Elijah, like Jeremiah, was a great prophet of God. One of my favorite Old Testament stories involves Elijah. It is found in 1 Kings 18. Elijah was fed up with the Israelite's worship of false gods, especially the god Baal. He issues a challenge on Mount Carmel. It is a classic battle of whose god reigns supreme. The prophets of Baal call on Baal to light the altar. They chant, scream, dance, and even cut themselves to get Baal's attention. Nothing happens. Elijah starts to rub it in a little and makes fun of them. He jokes that maybe Baal is asleep, on a journey, or using the bathroom. Baal's prophets give up, so it is Elijah's turn. He calls on God and something miraculous happens. Fire falls from Heaven and consumes everything on and near the altar. What a great victory for Elijah and the Israelites!

It is the best of times. It is also the worst of times. Consider the next chapter, 1 Kings 19. The wicked queen Jezebel is bloodthirsty for Elijah. She hates God and His prophets, especially Elijah. Does Elijah respond to her threats with courage and boldness? Does he stand up to her with faith and conviction? No. He tucks his tail in and runs. Elijah, according to **1 Kings 19:4**, "went a day's journey into the wilderness, and came and sat down under a juniper tree; and he requested for himself that he might die, and said, 'It is enough; now, O LORD, take my life, for I am no better than my fathers.' And he lay down and slept under a broom tree." Elijah, after a great victory on the mountain, finds himself in the valley of misery. He is so discouraged he wants to die. God responds to Elijah and sends help. He is prescribed food, water, and rest. Then Elijah hears from God and receives a new assignment. Even though Elijah was so down and discouraged he wanted to die, God still used him in a mighty way.

Some of the greatest followers of Christ have experienced depression. As mentioned earlier, both Martin Luther and Charles Spurgeon struggled with depression. Spurgeon saw depression as an indicator that God was about to use him for something great. C. S. Lewis, the author of "The Chronicles of Narnia," had bouts of depression. William Cowper was a poet and hymn writer. You may have heard his song *God Moves in Mysterious Ways*. Cowper struggled heavily with depression.

He even attempted to end his life by jumping off a bridge. God intervened and spared him.

If you are depressed, or have been depressed, you are in good company. Being depressed does not disqualify you from being used by God either. Sometimes God uses us in spite of our depression. Sometimes He uses us because of our depression. God wants us to live a life of joy. We also have real and raw emotions, including depression. When you are depressed, don't hide from the Bible, run to it. Don't feel condemned, feel comforted.

How to Use the Bible as Comfort

1. READ GOD'S GREAT PROMISES

He promises to take care of all your needs.

Jesus said, in **Matthew 6:25-26**, "For this reason I say to you, do not be worried about your life, as to what you will eat or what you will drink; nor for your body, as to what you will put on. Is not life more than food, and the body more than clothing? Look at the birds of the air, that they do not sow, nor reap nor gather into barns, and yet your heavenly Father feeds them. Are you not worth more than they?"

He promises to be faithful every day.

Lamentations 3:21-23, "This I call to my mind, therefore I have hope: The Lord's loving-kindness indeed never cease; for His compassions never fail. They are new every morning; great is Your faithfulness."

He promises to use all things for good.

Romans 8:28, "And we know that God causes all things to work together for good to those who love God, to those who are called according to His purpose."

The life of Joseph is a great example of this truth. Joseph's brothers sell him into slavery. He ends up in Egypt second only to Pharaoh. His brothers come to Egypt for food. They find themselves face to face with their brother. Joseph responds, in **Genesis 50:20**, "As for you, you meant evil against me, but God meant it for good in order to bring about this present result, to preserve many people alive." God is doing a work in your situation too. He can take anything and make it into something for your good and His glory.

He promises you will never go through something alone.

Hebrews 13:5, "Make sure your character is free from the love of money, being content with what you have; for He Himself has said, 'I will never desert you, nor will I forsake you.'" You may feel all alone, but God is with you.

He promises to make you better in times of trouble and hardship.

James 1:2-4, "Consider it all joy, my brethren, when you encounter various trials, knowing that the testing of your faith produces endurance. And let endurance have its perfect result, so that you may be perfect and complete, lacking in nothing." God uses the storms of life to build character and deepen your faith in Him.

He promises to care for your anxious heart and give you peace.

Philippians 4:4-7, "Rejoice in the Lord always; again I will say, rejoice! Let your gentle spirit be known to all men. The Lord is near. Be anxious for nothing, but in everything by prayer and supplication with thanksgiving let your requests be made known to God. And the peace of God, which surpasses all comprehension, will guard your hearts and your minds in Christ Jesus." Are you anxious? Take your burdens to God in prayer. He will listen and fill you with peace.

He promises, in Christ; to one day wipe away all our tears.

Revelation 21:4, "and He will wipe away every tear from their eyes; and there will no longer be any death; there will no longer be any mourning, nor crying, or pain; the first things have passed away." Your struggle may be for a moment, or it may be for a lifetime. It will not last an eternity!

2. USE THE BIBLE TO ATTACK DEPRESSIVE THOUGHTS

When you think no one cares, read how God cares.

The book of Exodus is a good place to start. Read how God delivered His people out of Egypt and provided their every need. From what has God delivered you? How has He taken care of your every need? Read the Gospels and see Jesus' love and compassion. Read how He died upon the cross for you. Since Jesus made that costly a sacrifice, consider how much He truly loves you. A great truth is found in **Romans 5:8**, "But God demonstrates His own love toward us, in that while we were yet sinners, Christ died for us."

When you are filled with worry, read how God takes care of you.

Read the Sermon on the Mount in Matthew. Jesus reminds us that the birds don't worry about food; neither do the fields worry about clothing. Why should you worry about life? God is watching over you and taking care of you.

When you think your problem is too big, read how God is bigger than all problems.

Moses and the Israelites were facing a dilemma. They were pinned in between the Egyptian army and the Red Sea. No way of escape seemed possible. God made a way by delivering them across the Red Sea. They had a big problem but an ever bigger God! David was facing a giant problem with Goliath. God was bigger than the giant was. Daniel was facing a giant problem in the lions' den. God was bigger than the ferocious lions.

Jesus lay in the grave. He had been beaten, betrayed, and crucified. God was bigger than that problem too. Jesus conquered death and rose from the dead. God is still the same God now as He was then. He is able to deliver you. It does not mean that

He will keep you from all harm. It does mean God is firmly in control. Whatever harm you do face, He is large and in charge.

When you feel like your cup is half empty, read how your cup runs over.

In **Psalm 23:5**, David says, "My cup overflows." Is your cup overflowing? Some see life from the perspective of a half empty cup. Others see it as half full. Maybe you feel like your cup has a crack in it. Just be glad you have a cup. Whatever you are facing in life, you can say with David, "My cup overflows. Surely goodness and mercy will follow me all the days of my life." God has blessed your life beyond measure.

When you feel useless, read how God uses us in times of weakness.

After Paul asks God to remove the thorn in his flesh three times, God says no. Pay attention to what happens next. Paul writes, in **2 Corinthians 12:9**, "And He has said to me, 'My grace is sufficient for you, for power is perfected in weakness.' Most gladly, therefore, I will boast all the more about my weaknesses, so that the power of Christ may dwell in me."

God manifests His strength through your weakness. If you feel weak and inadequate, that means you have to rely on the strength and might of God. Your weakness might be the only way God will use you. We cling to God and His strength when we are weak. When we are strong and think we have it all figured out, we tend to forget God and become self-sufficient.

When you feel overwhelmed with guilt, read about the forgiveness of God.

Paul wrote, in **Ephesians 1:7**, "In Him (Christ) we have redemption through His blood, the forgiveness of trespasses, according to the riches of His grace." In Christ, you have been forgiven of your sins. Don't let sin weigh you down, and don't let the guilt of your sin lead to further depression. Enjoy the forgiveness you have in Christ.

When you feel unworthy to be happy, read about your worth in Christ.

You may feel unworthy of a happy and healthy life. You may believe you deserve to be depressed. You are precious in God's sight and are of great value. You are worthy of a full and abundant life. Read Genesis 1. Genesis 1 teaches that we are made in the very image of God. Read Ephesians as well. It is a great reminder of who you are in Christ and what you have in Christ.

When you feel like you will never be happy, remember God can turn your mourning into dancing.

David wrote, in **Psalm 30:5**, "For His anger is but for a moment, His favor is for a lifetime; Weeping may last for the night, but a shout of joy comes in the morning." God can empower you to have joy no matter what.

3. READ AND PRAY THE PSALMS

I love the Psalms. They are rich with raw and true emotion. The Psalms speak to my heart. They will speak to yours as well. A specific Psalm may express exactly what you are feeling. As a result, reading the Psalms may help you identify feelings you are unable to describe or articulate. What brought comfort to the author of that specific Psalm can bring you comfort too.

A good way to enjoy the Psalms is to read and pray through a Psalm a day. I pick a Psalm from one of the Psalms of the day. The Psalms of the day are five Psalms based on the day of the week.[6] After choosing the five Psalms I narrow down my focus to one of those five Psalms. I focus on that one Psalm, either in its entirety, or a verse or two, as a guide for prayer and meditation. Here is the formula for choosing the five Psalms of the day: (1) Take the day's date as your first Psalm, (2) Add thirty to it for your second Psalm, (3) Add thirty to your second Psalm to get the third one, (4) Add thirty to your third Psalm for the fourth, and (5) Add thirty to your fourth Psalm to get the fifth one. Here is an example:

Today, as I write this, it is the 21st day of the month

1. 21
2. $21 + 30 = 51$
3. $51 + 30 = 81$
4. $81 + 30 = 111$
5. $111 + 30 = 141$

The Psalms of the day, for the 21st of the month are: 21, 51, 81, 111, and 141. The Psalms of the day for the 22nd would be: 22, 52, 82, 112, and 142. Choose one of the five Psalms, read and meditate upon it, and use it as a guide in your prayer life. You may want to focus on one verse, or several verses.

Consider Psalm 21 as an example. David, in verse one, declares that God gives the king strength. In addition, the king can greatly rejoice in God's salvation. You could pray, "Lord, I am not king, but

I am Your child. I am having a hard day today. Make me glad. Give me joy. I yearn to rejoice in Your salvation and praise You today."

4. MAINTAIN A STEADY DIET
OF GOD'S WORD

Reading the Bible daily is the best way to be comforted by its truths. It is through the word you learn who God is. It is through the word you learn to trust God. It is through the word you are comforted and grow in the faith. Peter wrote, in **1 Peter 2:2**, "Like newborn babies, long for the pure milk of the word, so that by it you may grow in respect to salvation." Do you long for the word? Are you reading it on a regular and consistent basis? Here are a few ideas for reading the Bible consistently:

☐ Take a book and read it several times, like John or 1st John, then choose another book.

☐ Read a Proverb a day. Read Proverbs 3 on the third of the month, for instance.

☐ Read and meditate on a Psalm a day.

☐ Read through the Bible in a year. You can access several good reading plans online.

Questions for reflection:

1. Are you reading the Bible on a consistent basis?

2. How would reading the Bible on a regular basis influence your life in a positive way?

Notes:

Chapter 5

SIX TIPS FOR SURVIVING DEPRESSION

Life is not like Disney World. Actually it is. My family went to Disney World a few years ago. My oldest daughter was overwhelmed with the rides, the characters, and the vibe of Disney. It is a fun and magical place; however, it was not a perfect trip by any means. It took about fourteen hours to drive there. It was hot. We had to wait in line at the rides. We walked multiple miles every day. I also toted a heavy backpack full of snacks and waters to save money. When we got home, after a long and exhausting trip, I noticed one of our luggage pieces was missing. I had left my daughter's luggage at the hotel. The Magical Kingdom is not all magic. It is expensive, hot, and stressful. Even while at Disney World I had to remind myself to focus on the positives and just enjoy the ride.

Life is a lot like Disney World. Life is magical. It is a blessing to be alive; however, life is not always easy. Trials, tribulations, and problems are a reality. We can choose to focus on the negatives and be overwhelmed. Or we can focus on the positives and enjoy the ride. For a time, my life seemed more like a castle of despair than a kingdom of magic. I was overwhelmed by all the negative things in my life. Just like that backpack, depression became a heavy burden to bear. I survived only by the grace of God. My life is not perfect. I still deal with depression periodically, but it usually does not linger long. I am now better equipped to handle it. The following are just a few lessons I have learned on my journey. I hope they are of help to you.

1. ADMIT YOU ARE DEPRESSED

You have to admit you are depressed to be victorious. It sounds so simple and obvious. Depression is a hard thing to admit, especially for men. It is also hard to recognize at times. Reading credible resources on depression will help you better understand its characteristics. Browsing reputable websites will be of benefit too. Above all, see a medical doctor. He or she can help diagnose your depression. It would also be wise to see a professional counselor.

2. GET HELP

I confess, "It was tough to admit I needed help."
It was even harder to make the effort to be helped. I
sought help from a medical doctor and a
professional counselor. Depression medication is a
common source of help. You may already be taking
medication for your depression. You may be
thinking about taking it. Should you take depression
medication? That is a decision you, your family,
and your doctor need to make. I took depression
medication for a season. It helped me through the
darkest of times. The medication gave me the extra
boost I needed to fight my depression. I stopped
taking the medication once I dealt with the root
issues.

Some people will need to take medication for a
longer period than I did. Maybe you can survive
without it. Never get off your medication without
your doctor's consent. Do your research. As with
anything, there are benefits and drawbacks. Again,
the decision is up to you, your family, and your
doctor. I believe medicine is a gift of God. He is the
Great Physician. I believe He can heal. I also
believe He can use modern medicine to heal our
minds and bodies. Don't be ashamed if you have to
take medication. People take medication for high
blood pressure. Why can't you take medication for

depression? Whatever you do, get help. Here are some places to seek out help:

- Friends/Family
- Doctor
- Counselor/Psychiatrist/Psychologist
- Pastor

3. TELL OTHERS ABOUT IT

You need to tell others about your depression. That may not be easy for you, but it is needed. If you are married, tell your spouse. If you are a child, tell a parent. Tell a friend, a coworker, or someone at church you can trust. You do not need to go through depression alone. I initially told my wife and a few close friends. It took me a few years to tell my parents. It took even longer to tell my church. I wish I had shared more openly in the beginning of my depression. Telling others provides relief and support. It also provides opportunities for you to help and encourage others dealing with depression.

4. TELL GOD ABOUT IT

Prayer is essential to battling depression. Set aside time every day to pray. Tell God how you really feel. Be honest. Maybe you struggle in your prayer life. I struggle at times too. Try writing out your prayers. Or pray the Psalms, as mentioned in the previous chapter. Use the Lord's Prayer as another bow in your quiver. People often recite the Lord's Prayer word for word. Jesus intended it to be more of a model of prayer than exact words to repeat. Consider the example of how you might use the Lord's Prayer for your depression:

Matthew 6:9-13

Our Father who is in Heaven

"Thank you for being my Father. I know You love me and care for me. Help me enjoy a rich and intimate relationship with You. Your being in Heaven is a reminder that life here on earth is temporary. Everything I am depressed about will not last an eternity. I must keep my eyes on You."

Hallowed be Your name

"Let people see how great and awesome You are. I know that You can even use my depression to set apart and exalt Your name."

Your Kingdom come, Your will be done, on earth as it is in Heaven

"Help me stop trying to be king. Take over the throne of my heart. Rule and reign in my life. I pray for Your will to be done in the midst of my depression. I surrender all."

Give us this day our daily bread

"Thank you for providing my physical needs. I need more than physical food right now. I need food for my soul. I need to be nourished emotionally and mentally. Give me all that I need for today."

And forgive us our debts

"God, I know I need to be forgiven. Though my depression may not be a sin, it has resulted in my sinning against you. It has caused me to be bitter, angry, and self-centered. It has caused me to doubt You. It has caused me to push others away from my life. Forgive me. Rid me of my guilt and shame. Since You have and will forgive me, I can now forgive myself."

As we have also forgiven our debtors

"Help me to forgive those who have mistreated me. Help me to forgive those who have caused pain to my life. Help me not to hold a grudge towards anyone. As You have forgiven me, help me in turn forgive others."

And do not lead us into temptation, but deliver us from evil

"Sometimes my depression has led me into temptation. I am tempted to complain. I am tempted to not trust You. I am tempted not to care about others. Help me not to go down the path of sin. Help me to follow You no matter what. Protect me from evil and the evil one. I know I cannot blame Satan for everything, but spiritual warfare is real. I am in the midst of a battle between good and evil. Sometimes I feel defeated. Thank you for the deliverance Christ has provided on the cross. He is victorious. Help me to experience that in a real and personal way."

For Yours is the kingdom and the power and the glory forever. Amen.

5. EDUCATE YOURSELF

Imagine you are chosen to be on Jeopardy. You are told the show will focus on art, Shakespeare, and European history. How would you respond? You would probably start studying art, Shakespeare, and

European history. Isn't your life more important than being on Jeopardy? Isn't your mental health more valuable than winning a few thousand dollars? Study the subject of depression. Educate yourself and be empowered. I sought answers when I realized I was depressed. I read numerous books on depression. I also read online articles. You may not feel like reading or doing research, but it will be of great benefit to you.

> *Prayer is essential to battling depression.*

I learned what causes depression. I learned the link between diet and depression. I learned how my thoughts affect my feelings. I learned how fish oil medication has been proven to help with depression.[7] I learned how exercise relieves depression. The more I learned about depression, the more I felt empowered and equipped to handle it.

Seek good and credible resources. Ask a counselor for a list of good books, both secular and spiritual. Seek advice from a depression survivor you respect. Talk to your pastor too. He may be aware of some resources. Become an expert in the causes and remedies of depression. With your knowledge of depression, you'll be able to help others as they struggle with depression.

6. KEEP A JOURNAL

Don't worry guys. A journal is not a pink diary with a lock on it. It is simply a way to write your daily activities, feelings, and struggles. Perhaps you are comfortable with a word processing program. You may prefer using old fashioned pen and paper. Journal programs are available online as well. Use whatever method works best for you. For each entry write the date and whatever is on your mind and heart. Here are a few prompters to begin a journal entry:

• Today, I felt good about…

• I am really stressed about…

• God has reminded me today of His…

• On a scale of 1-10, my depression/anxiety today is at a …

• I can praise God because…

• The most important thing I will remember about today is…

• The most important thing I want to accomplish today is…

You can add your own examples. Journaling is simply a way to express what is on your heart and mind. Don't worry about the grammar, sentence structure, or what words to use. Just start writing. Writing is very therapeutic. Over time you can go back and read about your past struggles and triumphs. You can also be reminded of God's faithfulness in your life. Here is an example of one of my journal entries:

November 16, 2005, "Yesterday was a decent day. I had a somewhat productive time studying and preparing the sermon for Sunday. In the evening, I spent a little time with Lori and Houdini (my Jack-Russell Terrier dog). I am in a stage now to where I don't seem to feel connected to real life, and I don't know who I am. It seems strange but it seems that everything in my life is so dramatically different than it was just a few years ago. What is life anyway? Does everyone feel this way? Does each one seem to just be marking their days and yearning for something else? Life seems to be a blur, a great mystery."

Here is another entry dated *April 4, 2006*, "Yesterday was a good day. I seemed sluggish and ineffective at work, and I began the day slowly and unproductive. My devotions were deficient as well. But, as the day went on, the fire of Holy Scripture warmed my soul. In the evening, I spent some time with my sweet wife."

The first entry seems very depressing, but it is a look into my soul at that very moment. The next entry is a little more positive. It is a reminder that someone can have a positive day in the midst of depression. Every emotion of every day serves a purpose to draw us closer to God and make us more like Christ. A journal provides access to your feelings over the course of several years. You can read about the good, the bad, and ugly.

Questions for reflection:

1. Have you even admitted to yourself that you are depressed?

2. What is keeping you from getting help?

3. Whom do you need to tell about your battle with depression?

4. What do you know about depression? What should you know?

5. Have you ever considered starting a journal?
   What would it take for you to begin one today?

Notes:

Chapter 6

FIVE MORE TIPS FOR
SURVIVING DEPRESSION

In 2013, a man was lost in the woods of Northern California for seventeen days. Gene Penaflor, 72 years of age, was lost while deer hunting. He survived by eating lizards, frogs, and squirrels. Gene also had to deal with the snow and freezing temperatures. What would you do if you were lost in the woods? Would you eat lizards, frogs, and squirrels?

You are far more likely to survive such an event with a survival kit. A survival kit contains essentials such as matches, a compass, and flares. Depression is like being in the woods. You lose your way, and it gets dark and scary. Instead of eating lizards, frogs, and squirrels, you feast on worry, fear, and stress. You need a Depression Survival Kit. I carry one with me all the time. I do not mean a literal kit of course. I am referring to certain habits and resources to incorporate into your daily life. What should be in your survival kit? The previous chapter listed six essential items: 1. Admit you are depressed, 2. Get help, 3. Tell others about it, 4. Pray and tell God about it, 5. Educate yourself, and 6. Keep a journal. I would include five more items.

1. EXERCISE

Exercise is good for you. It is not just good for your body; it is good for your emotions too. Studies reveal that exercise is an anti-depressant. If you exercise regularly you "are at much lower risk for depression than couch potatoes."[8] Exercise allows your mind and body to be better equipped to battle stress and depression. Perhaps you could bicycle, swim, strength train, dance, or run. Consider the benefits of exercise:

- It provides relief from stress
- It keeps you physically fit
- It gives you a goal to pursue
- It is a good distraction in tough times
- It can be a good way to connect with others

I confess, "Exercise is a big stress reliever for me." It has been a key ingredient to my surviving depression. My exercise of choice is running. I began running while in seminary. I ran a few 5K races (3.1 miles). I then set my sights on a huge goal, running a full marathon (26.2 miles). I completed my first marathon in 2008. It was a huge accomplishment for me. It helped me physically, emotionally, and spiritually.

I recently completed my seventh full marathon. I have also completed a couple of triathlons. A triathlon is a race comprised of swimming, bicycling, and running. I also had a life-long dream of taking martial arts, so I took Tae Kwon Do for a season. I live a very busy and hectic life, but I find time to exercise. You don't have to complete a marathon or take martial arts. Do something. Keep moving. Enjoy life!

2. STAY POSITIVE

"You are what you eat" is a well-known saying. I guess I am a peanut butter and jelly sandwich. It is more accurate to say, "You are what you think." Think about your thoughts. If your thoughts are primarily negative, you will be affected in a negative way. If your thoughts are primarily positive, you will be affected in a positive way. It is the old glass half full or half empty theory. How do you see things? What is your perspective? It is important to get a handle on your thoughts. Depression is often associated with stinking thinking. Consider what thoughts someone with depression may dwell on:

• I am hopeless

• I am unworthy

• I cannot do anything

• I am miserable

• No one cares about me

• This is the worst day ever

• I hate my life

If this is a picture of your thought life, you can see why you may be stuck in a rut of depression. How we feel is "caused by what we tell ourselves about our circumstances, whether in words or attitudes."[9] Consider **Philippians 4:8**, "Finally, brethren, whatever is true, whatever is honorable, whatever is right, whatever is pure, whatever is lovely, whatever is of good repute, if there is any excellence and if anything worthy of praise, dwell on these things." Instead of dwelling on the negative, focus on whatever is:

☐ True

☐ Honorable

☐ Right

☐ Pure

☐ Lovely

☐ Of Good Repute

☐ Excellent

☐ Worthy of Praise

Imagine you are having an awful day. You feel like all is lost. There is no hope whatsoever. Ask yourself, "Is that true? Is there really no hope?" The truth is there is always hope in Christ. So focus on what is true. Perhaps you are depressed because your spouse or children do not meet your expectations. Focus on what is lovely and excellent about your spouse. Think about what is honorable about your children. Practicing a Philippians 4:8 mindset will be of great benefit. Here is another helpful exercise. Ask yourself a few questions at the end of the day. The questions can help you become more positive. Here are a few examples to consider:

☐ What was the best thing that happened to me today?

☐ How has God blessed me today?

☐ For what am I most thankful for in my life?

☐ What did I do today that I am proud of?

☐ Who showed me love and kindness today?

Here is a neat exercise referred to as the "What-Went-Well Exercise," also known as "Three Blessings."[10]

> Every night for the next week, set aside ten minutes before you go to sleep. Write down three things that went well today and why they went well. You may use a journal on your computer to write about the events, but it is important to have a physical record of what you wrote. The three things need not be earthshaking in importance ("My husband picked up my favorite ice cream for dessert on the way home from work today"), but they can be important ("My sister just gave birth to a healthy baby boy").
>
> Next to each positive event, answer the question, "Why did this happen?" For example, if you wrote that your husband picked up ice cream, write, "Because my husband is really thoughtful sometimes" or "because I remembered to call him from work and reminded him to stop by the grocery store." Or if you wrote, "My sister

just gave birth to a healthy baby boy," you might pick as the cause… "She did everything right during her pregnancy."

Writing about the positive events in your life may seem awkward at first, but stick with it for a while. It gets easier.

3. SEARCH YOUR SOUL

Have you ever seen your vehicle's check engine light come on? It is a sign that something is not quite right. Depression is sometimes your body's warning signal. It is your check engine light, a warning that something is not quite right. Perhaps you have been overly stressed. If so, find a way to deal with it in a healthy and positive way. Perhaps you have inward anger. Find out why and take care of it. Perhaps you have not properly grieved a loss. Grieve the loss. It may hurt for a while, but it will help you heal.

I had to deal with stress, anger, and especially grief. **I confess, "I am not good at grieving."** I had to take time and intentionally grieve my losses. It helped get me on the right track to mental health. One way to begin the grieving process is take "a day away on a retreat with God to journey and pray about significant events in your past that, perhaps, you have not grieved. Give yourself permission to feel."[11] From my own experience, a personal retreat is beneficial to restore hope and healing.

4. REALIZE YOUR TRUE WORTH

Depression makes you seem worthless. You may lack confidence or even feel like a failure. You may think you are not worthy of happiness. People typically base self-worth on the three "A's."

☐ Achievements – what have they achieved in life, how successful they are …

☐ Accumulations – what car they drive, what type of house they own…

☐ Attractiveness – what they look like, how much they weigh…

One's self-worth is not based on any of the above accolades. Self-worth is based on who you are in Christ. Read the book of Ephesians. In Ephesians, Paul emphasizes who we are in Christ. It is a great book to help boost your self-worth. After you read it, read it again. Just consider all you have in Christ. You are:

• In Christ, **Ephesians 1:1**

• Blessed with every spiritual blessing, **Ephesians 1:3**

- Adopted into the family of God, **Ephesians 1:4-6**

- Redeemed and forgiven of your sins, **Ephesians 1:7**

- Sealed with the Holy Spirit, **Ephesians 1:13-14**

- Blessed with hope, spiritual riches, and God's power, **Ephesians 1:18-19**

- Saved from your sins and spiritually alive, **Ephesians 2:1-10**

- Brought near to Christ and at peace with Him, **Ephesians 2:13-14**

- Given access to the very presence of God, **Ephesians 2:18**

- Deeply loved by Christ, **Ephesians 3:14-20**

- Blessed and gifted to be in a local church, **Ephesians 4:7-16**

- No longer in darkness, but part of the light, **Ephesians 5:8**

- Blessed to be filled by the Holy Spirit, **Ephesians 5:18**

- Given all the resources you need for spiritual warfare, **Ephesians 6:10-20**

This is just a taste of all you have in Christ. You are a person of great worth. Ephesians is a reminder that your value comes from Christ, not your looks or monetary wealth. Your identity is not based on your family or education. It is not tied to your past, no matter how unpleasant. It is based on who you are in Christ. You may feel like a total failure, but you are not. You are a person of great value in Christ. You are blessed beyond measure and worthy of joy. Find your identity and joy in Christ.

> *Self-worth is based on who you are in Christ.*

5. CANCEL YOUR PITY PARTY

The best thing I ever did was cancel my pity party. Have you ever thrown a pity party? It is a great time to moan and complain. It is certainly not a way to improve your mood. Paul wrote, in **Philippians 2:14-15**, "Do all things without grumbling or disputing; so that you will prove yourselves to be blameless and innocent, children of God approve reproach in the midst of a crooked and perverse generation, among whom you appear as lights in the world." It is hard to be a good witness when you grumble, gripe, and complain. It is certainly hard to feel better too.

Part of not grumbling is refusing to throw a pity party. Cancel your pity party. Burst the balloons. Throw away the cake. Cancel the clown and shut it down. No one likes to attend pity parties anyway. It is so easy to feel sorry for ourselves. It only worsens the situation. It doesn't mean not to grieve your loss or feel the pain of depression. It does mean you refuse to have an Eeyore attitude and think, "Poor old me." When I find myself spiraling into a state of depression, I try to cancel all pity parties. I am not making light of your circumstances, or why you are depressed; however, don't make your time of depression harder than it needs to be.

Questions for reflection:

1. How could you get a little exercise? How would exercise benefit your life?

2. Do your thoughts tend to be negative or positive?

3. Is there something you need to grieve?

4. What is your value based on? Is it Christ or something/someone else?

5. Do you find yourself throwing pity parties?
   Do they help?

Notes:

Chapter 7

HOW DEPRESSION IS A BLESSING

I confess, "Depression can be a blessing." It seems odd, but the Bible teaches that God is at work in every situation. Paul wrote, in **Romans 8:28**, "And we know that God causes all things to work together for good to those who love God, to those who are called according to His purpose." God can turn your lemons into lemonade, even depression. The Bible also teaches that suffering is for our good. God uses it to develop our character and draw us closer to Him. James writes, in **James 1:2**, "Consider it all joy, my brethren, when you encounter various trials." How can we count depression joy? James tells us in **James 1:3-4**, "Knowing that the testing of your faith produces endurance. And let endurance have its perfect result, so that you may be perfect and complete, lacking in nothing." Hard times develop our faith and produce endurance and maturity. Some of the greatest lessons in life come in times of trials and tribulations. Some of the sweetest times with God are during trials and tribulations.

As mentioned earlier, Joseph's brothers despise the relationship he has with his father, so they sell him into slavery. He eventually oversees Potiphar's house. Joseph is thrown in prison after Potiphar's wife falsely accuses him. A few years later Joseph interprets one of Pharaoh's dreams. He is released from prison and given an important position in Egypt. Joseph oversees Egypt's grain supply during a severe famine. Everyone benefits from Joseph's leadership, even his wicked brothers. If Joseph was never sold into slavery, he would have never been in that position. Lives would not have been saved. Here are a few questions for you to ponder: What is the worst thing that ever happened to Joseph? What is the best thing that ever happened to Joseph? Both require the same answer.

God is a master weaver, weaving the stories of our lives. Trials and tribulations are often intertwined with blessings. You may not understand what He is doing, but He is doing things for your good and His glory. Depression is terrible. God has allowed it in your life for a reason. It is making you more like Christ. You are learning lessons about who you are and who Christ is. Like Joseph, it may be the worst thing you have ever gone through.

When all is said and done, it may be one of the best things that has happened. Consider the *Confederate's Prayer*.

I asked God for strength, that I might achieve, I was made weak, that I might learn humbly to obey.

I asked for health, that I might do great things, I was given infirmity, that I might do better things.

I asked for riches, that I might be happy, I was given poverty, that I might be wise.

I asked for power, that I might have the praise of men, I was given weakness, that I might feel the need of God.

I asked for all things, that I might enjoy life, I was given life, that I might enjoy all things.

I got nothing that I asked for, but everything I had hoped for.

Almost despite myself, my unspoken prayers were answered.

I am, among all men, most richly blessed.[12]

> *Trials and tribulations are often intertwined with blessings.*

God has great and precious blessings for His children. The blessings are not always in bright and shiny packages. Sometimes they present themselves during dark and weary times. Everyone wants to be on the mountain. It is often in the valley where we find a rich and meaningful walk with God. For me, depression was a dark and weary valley. Looking back I see how it was really a time of blessing as well. I am a far better person because of my depression. Here are 10 blessings I received because of depression:

10 BLESSINGS OF MY DEPRESSION

1. I Learned to Take Better Care of Myself

Depression has reminded me of the importance of eating healthy, exercising, and properly handling stress.

2. I Learned to Express my Feelings

I typically hold my emotions in. Depression has taught me to express my feelings instead. When I am anxious, for instance, I feel more comfortable telling my wife.

3. I Learned to Grieve my Losses

Depression often stems from loss. Grieving may be an essential part of working through your depression. I once set apart a day and withdrew from my daily distractions. I went to a park and spent time alone with God. I wrote down the losses in my life. I wrote down the death of my father, my difficult time in ministry, and other areas of loss. Acknowledging my losses brought relief to my weary soul. Perhaps you could do the same.

4. I Learned to Better Deal with Anger

Depression can sometimes stem from inward anger. Holding anger in can smother your soul and grieve your spirit. I had to learn to deal with my anger in a healthy way. It has not been an easy lesson, and I still have much improvement to make.

5. I Learned to Fight for Joy

Christ wants us to be people of joy. Joy is not automatic. You have to fight for it. Depression has taught me to fight for joy. Pursuing Christ is the only path to true joy. One of my favorite verses is **Psalm 16:11**, in which David wrote, "You will make known to me the path of life; in Your presence is fullness of joy; in Your right hand there are pleasures forever." True pleasure and joy is not found in the things of this world, but in God and Christ. Pursue Christ and fight for joy!

6. I Learned to Sympathize with Others

When I hear of others struggling with depression, I quickly identify with them. Instead of being judgmental and wondering what is wrong with them, I feel their pain. My sympathy is not limited to depression. I have not dealt with many of the issues others have, but I have been through my own times of darkness and weakness. It makes it easier for me to listen and truly care.

7. I Learned to Focus on the Good Things in Life

Are you having a good day or a bad one? Is your life blessed or is it a mess? It depends on how you look at things. If you look for negative things you will see life in a negative way. If you look for positive things you will see life in a positive way. Depression can cause you to see all of life in a negative light. I had to learn to focus on the good things in life. It doesn't mean we ignore what is wrong or what needs to be corrected. It means we decide to dwell on what is good and of God.

8. I Learned to Endure the Hard Times

Not everything in life is a mountain top experience. Sometimes we live in the valley. Vince Lombardi, the legendary coach of the Green Bay Packers said, "It does not matter how many times you get knocked down, but how many times you get up." Depression is a punch to the gut, but it does not have to be a knockout punch. I have learned not to let it keep me down.

Whatever hardship you are facing, keep on keeping on. Be like the little engine that could. He kept telling himself, "I think I can. I think I can." My pressing on in the face of depression has given me the wisdom and stamina to press on in the face of other obstacles as well. I don't remember where I read this, but it is a great reminder. Take the d, e, and i out of depression and what do you have? Press on!

Depression

~~De~~ press ~~i~~ on

If you can press on and endure depression, just imagine what else you could endure. Hard times make us better and more apt for the hard times yet to come.

9. I Learned I was Fragile and Needed God

I have been blessed with physical health thus far. My issue has been mental health. Being gripped with depression has been a humbling experience. It is a great reminder that, though I may be relatively young and healthy, I am still fragile and in need of God.

10. I Learned God's Grace is Sufficient

God's grace is sufficient no matter how bad things get. He is all we need. God can even turn depression into a blessing. It doesn't mean we should pray to be depressed, or seek ways to enter into depression. It means depression is never in vain. You will be richly blessed because of your struggles and sleepless nights. God is using depression to make you more like Christ and draw you closer to Him. You are becoming all God wants because of, not in spite of, your depression. Don't let it make you bitter, let it make you better!

Questions for reflection:

1. Can you think of one way depression has enriched your life?

2. How has depression made you a better person?

3. Has depression drawn you closer to God or further away from God?

4. Do you believe God can use depression for your good and His glory?

Notes:

Chapter 8

IF YOU HAVE A DEPRESSED FAMILY MEMBER

Depression is never a one way street. It affects more than the one depressed. It affects family and loved ones too. Depression affects marriages. It affects parent and child relationships. It affects sibling relationships. A depressed person tends to withdraw from intimacy. A depressed person might be angry or irritable as well. Sometimes it is difficult to communicate with someone who is depressed. For family members who have never been depressed, it may be hard to understand why their loved one is depressed. Care and concern needs to be given not only to the depressed, but also to his or her family. An article from Psychology Today notes:

> Depression is not just a medical matter. It's a family one, too. The behaviors and mood of a depressed person affects the whole

family. There's the irritability, which sets off conflicts and derails family dynamics. The negative thought patterns, which become a prism of pessimism for everyone. The withdrawal that literally disrupts relationships and breeds wholesale feelings of rejection. There are major responsibilities that get displaced. There is a general burden of stress.

And yet, families can be major forces of care, comfort, even cure. They are crucial to proper recognition and treatment of the disorder, not just at the beginning but throughout. They are the de facto caregivers, willingly or not. They contribute powerfully to the emotional atmosphere the depressed person inhabits, and so can be agents of recovery... Yes, depression has a huge impact on families. And families have a huge impact on depression.[13]

I confess, "Depression greatly impacted my family." I am blessed to have a loving and patient wife. She put up with a lot when I was depressed. Some weeks, and even months, I withdrew into a shell. I was sad, quiet, and irritable. While we had a good marriage during those times, it was not as healthy as it could have been. We had trouble communicating. I was probably not a fun person to be with at times. Because I was depressed, I was not giving her my all. I have asked my wife to share a little about the struggles and challenges she faced as a result of my depression.

Me: "What was the hardest thing for you in my time of depression?"

Lori: "It was difficult because I didn't feel like there was anything I could do to make you happy. I didn't know what to do to bring you out of it. I wanted to make things better for you, and I could not do that. It didn't matter what I did. I was afraid the depression would get so bad that it would overtake you to the point of no return. All I wanted to do was get you out of it, and I didn't know what to do."

Me: "It sounds like you felt helpless in the situation. Why?"

Lori: "I felt like no matter what I did you were still going to be sad and upset. No matter what I did, I could not make it better. So I felt like a failure at times."

Me: "How did my depression affect our relationship?"

Lori: "It was hard because little things upset you more than normal. I felt like I was doing something wrong. I felt I was to blame because I could not make you happy. I wondered what I had done to make you depressed. Your depression also made communication a challenge because you did not want to open up and talk."

Me: "Can you see any benefit that has derived from my depression?"

Lori: "There were times when you did open up, and it drew us closer together. Going through the depression has allowed you to help others struggling with depression. Your experience lets them know they are not by themselves. I feel like you overcoming depression is a major milestone."

Me: "What advice would you give to someone who has a depressed family member?"

Lori: "You have to just continue to pray and ask God to lead him or her out of it. Secondly, no matter how hard it may get, and no matter how many times you want to give up, you need to continue to show support and love. Let him or her know that you are there no matter what."

Lori's most pressing issue was feeling helpless. She wanted to help but didn't know how. Perhaps, like Lori, you have a loved one struggling with depression. If you have depressed family members here are some do's and don'ts:

Do's & Don'ts for Dealing with Depressed Family Members

Don't tell them to snap out of it and get on with life.
Do try to understand what they are feeling and why.

If they could just snap out of the depression they would. It is not that easy. Communicate with them and try to understand why they are depressed. Just being available and attentive to their needs will be a great benefit.

Don't tell them they lack faith in God.
Do spend time praying with them and for them.

Depression is typically not a result of a lack of faith. Dedicated followers of Christ have struggled and do struggle with depression. Instead of being a source of discouragement, spend time praying with them and for them.

Don't make fun of them or add to their shame.
Do encourage them to get help.

People dealing with depression might have shame as a result. Don't add fuel to the fire. Be an encourager and someone they can count on. You may be the only one who can guide them to help.

Don't harass or badger them into sharing.
Do let them know you are there for them.

Sometimes people don't feel like sharing their feelings. It is especially true of the depressed. It is important to open up and share, but there are times when people are not comfortable with it. Don't force the issue. Let them know you are available and give them the space they need. Hopefully, in time they will open up and share their struggles.

> *Be an encourager and*
> *someone they can count on.*

Don't think you are unaffected by their depression.
Do see how depression affects you.

You have a responsibility to care for your depressed family member. Depression affects you as well. You also have a responsibility to care for yourself.

If you are worn out emotionally, physically, and/or mentally, you will not be of much help. Make sure you get plenty of rest. Spend time praying for your family member. Be a part of a local church and small group Bible study. Your church and small group should be a source of great encouragement and support.

Questions for reflection:

1. Do you have any depressed family members?

2. How has depression affected your family?

3. What can you do to maintain family health and intimacy?

Notes:

Chapter 9

WHAT CHURCHES NEED TO DO

It has been said that the church is a hospital for sinners, not a museum for saints. **I confess, "It is true in theory, but not so much in reality."** For churches, Halloween is not once a year, but rather every Sunday morning. People go to church with masks on. Not literal masks of course, but they wear "masks" pretending to be something or someone they are not. Some wear the mask of having a perfect marriage and a perfect family. Others wear the mask of being a super Christian who never struggles with prayer or Bible study. A few wear the mask of judge, looking down on others. As a result, it is often difficult to come to church and admit you have a problem.

It is not easy to tell your small group you are struggling with sin. It is especially challenging to tell your church family about your depression. The depressed person may feel shame. Perhaps some in the congregation believe depression is either a sin or a result of weak faith. As a result, the depressed often wear a mask too. They come to church pretending all is well, but they are dying on the inside. I have been a pastor for numerous years and in numerous places. The reality is that everyone in the church has problems.

No perfect marriage exists. No perfect family exists. Christians struggle with being holy and devoted. Devoted believers battle anger, lust, and greed. Everyone has problems and pain. In every congregation there are probably several people struggling with depression. Churches need to stop being so superficial. Believers need to peel away the masks and be open and honest about their struggles, sins, and sadness. When someone's depression is mentioned in the church, people tend to respond by:

<u>Pretending</u> all is well and no one is depressed

<u>Minimizing</u> it as if it is not a big deal

<u>Judging</u> it as if the person is living in sin

<u>Spiritualizing</u> it by telling the depressed to snap out of it and have faith in God

I am a pastor of a local church, so I love the church. Jesus loves the church and died for the church. Don't abandon it; however, it is not a perfect place. The church must do a better job to help the hurting. We need to put the stones away and help one another out. Instead of throwing rocks to knock others down, we need to throw a rope to help them up. Someone observed, "Our job as Christian leaders is not to throw rocks, but to throw ropes. We need to spend more time edifying one another and less time classifying one another."[14]

Do you throw a rope or a rock? When others are down, whether it is depression or some other issue, it is tempting to tear them down rather than build them up. You and I are called to be encouragers. **Ephesians 4:29** reminds us, "Let no unwholesome word proceed from your mouth, but only such a word as is good for edification according to the need of the moment, so that it will give grace to those who hear." We need to encourage those in pain, especially in times of depression.

I am a Southern Baptist and the pastor of a Southern Baptist church. Each year the Southern Baptist Convention is held. Decisions are made, controversies are addressed, and resolutions are declared. In 2013, a resolution on mental health was made. It is a lengthy statement, but a great resource.

It sheds much light on depression for believers and the local church. I hope it is of benefit to you. The resolution is as follows:

On Mental Health Concerns and the Heart of God[15]

WHEREAS, God made all things perfectly good in design for His glory and the good of humanity (Genesis 1–2); and

WHEREAS, Adam and Eve rebelled against Him, choosing their own way and the way of the Evil One, and consequently ushered sin and disorder into our world and the whole human race (Genesis 3; Romans 5:12–21; 8:22); and

WHEREAS, As a consequence of this Fall, humanity is subjected to many kinds of mental health problems including autism spectrum disorders; intellectual disability; mental health conditions like schizophrenia, clinical depression, anxiety disorders, bipolar disorders, and eating disorders; and diseases of the aged such as dementia and Alzheimer's disease; and

WHEREAS, God did not abandon fallen humanity but loved the world (John 3:16–

17) and launched a plan of redemption—a restoration that is incomplete in this age but will be perfected in heaven (1 Peter 1:3–9); and

WHEREAS, Those with mental health concerns, like all people, are crowned with honor and dignity, being made in the image and likeness of God (Psalm 8:4–6; James 3:9); and

WHEREAS, Those with mental health concerns are disproportionately represented among the homeless and in our correctional systems, indicating a tragic neglect of these persons who are made in God's image; and

WHEREAS, Those who are struggling with mental health concerns often feel isolated, stigmatized, and rejected, sometimes resorting to self-destructive behaviors, including suicide; and

WHEREAS, Suicide is a tragedy, leaving heartache, pain, and unanswered questions in its wake; and

WHEREAS, Recent events in our nation and among God's people have underscored the tragedy of mental health concerns and their devastating toll within our families, our churches, and our culture; and

WHEREAS, Jesus Christ spent time with and healed some of the most marginalized members of the culture of His day; and

WHEREAS, God has appointed His people to be the main representatives of His heart and values to the world; and

WHEREAS, God has called us to share the Gospel of Christ with all people, including those suffering various mental health concerns; now, therefore, be it

RESOLVED, That the messengers to the Southern Baptist Convention meeting in Houston, Texas, on June 11–12, 2013, affirm that those with mental health concerns are of immeasurable value to God; and be it further

RESOLVED, That the mission Jesus described as His own in Luke 4:18-19 should also be the mission of His church, namely to proclaim liberty to those who are oppressed by means of godly biblical counsel; and be it further

RESOLVED, That we commit to affirm, support, and share God's love and redemption with those with mental health concerns; and be it further

RESOLVED, That we oppose all stigmatization and prejudice against those who are suffering from mental health concerns; and be it further

RESOLVED, That we support the wise use of medical intervention for mental health concerns when appropriate; and be it further

RESOLVED, That we support research and treatment of mental health concerns when undertaken in a manner consistent with a biblical worldview; and be it further

RESOLVED, That families who have lost a member to suicide deserve great care, concern, and compassion from Christians and their churches, including the assurance that those in Christ cannot be separated from the eternal love of God that is in Christ Jesus; and be it finally

RESOLVED, That we call on all Southern Baptists and our churches to look for and create opportunities to love and minister to, and develop methods and resources to care for, those who struggle with mental health concerns and their families.

I applaud the Southern Baptist Convention for taking a stand. All churches, regardless of denomination or tradition, must take a similar stand.

WHAT CHURCHES NEED TO DO

1. Admit Mental Health is an Issue

People in the pews are struggling. Local churches can no longer turn a blind eye. Churches must realize depression is a reality that needs to be addressed. The ones dealing with depression need to be ministered to, as do the affected family members.

2. Acknowledge Depression is Not a Sin

Churches need to acknowledge that depression is not a sin. Depressed church members no longer need to live in shame. Church members need to learn how to reach out to the depressed with love and support rather than contempt and judgment.

> *People in the pews are struggling.*

3. Provide a Safe and Loving Place for the Depressed

Perhaps a church could start a support group for the depressed. It would be a great way for them to feel supported and connected to the church. It would also be a great outlet for them to share their struggles. Most churches are not mega-churches with unlimited resources. Not every church can respond in the same manner.

If anything local churches could communicate the reality of depression via sermons and newsletters, for example. The better informed church members are, the more likely the depressed will feel welcome and comfortable admitting their depression. Not only that, church members will be better equipped as to how to minister to those who are depressed within the church family, as well as their own family.

4. Teach the Truths of Scripture Regarding Depression

Perhaps the pastor could preach a series of sermons on depression. Perhaps a small group could go through a six week study on depression, for instance. Churches must respond to the people in the pews. It is time to step up and do something. If the depressed cannot find encouragement at their church, what does that say about the church? What does that say about our love for one another?

Paul wrote, in **Galatians 6:2**, "Bear one another's burdens." Depression is most certainly a burden. We are all in this together. The church must be a place the depressed can seek refuge and restoration. Don't be discouraged if you feel your church is not a place of refuge for you and your depression. **I confess, "As I consider this great need, I too must do more in my church."** So don't give up. Perhaps God has you at your church to improve your church's awareness of the needs of the depressed.

Questions for reflection:

1. What has been your church's response to depression?

2. How could you help your church minister to the depressed?

Notes:

Conclusion

HOW TO FIND TRUE JOY

Dedicated Christians suffer with depression. God is good all the time, yet we live in a fallen world. We have periods of sadness and depression. God promises us, in **Revelation 21:4** to "wipe away every tear from their eyes; and there will no longer be any death; neither shall there be any mourning, or crying, or pain, the first things have passed away." God certainly does comfort us here on earth, but this promise will find its ultimate fulfillment in Heaven. **I confess, "I cannot wait to fully enjoy this promise."** God is the God of all comfort. He does bring peace; yet, this world is filled with pain and suffering. How can we find true joy?

If you know Christ, and truly follow Him, turn to Him for comfort. He is your Shepherd to guide you through the valley of the shadow of depression. If you don't know Christ, give Him your life. When you submit to Him as Lord and King you will not be free of problems. Your depression may not disappear; however, you will find hope for your life. He will give you peace and joy, regardless of your circumstances. He will forgive you of your sins and provide a home for you in Heaven.

The Bible says all have sinned and fall short of God's glory. We have missed His mark, which is perfection. No one is good enough to get to Heaven. No one can do enough good things. The only way to be right with God is through Christ. He died on the cross for you. He took the punishment for your sins. Turn from your sins and turn to Christ. Give Him your life. Then and only then will you find true and everlasting joy. Get involved in a local church. Spend time reading the Bible and praying to God. Consider reading and thinking about:

John 3:16
John 14:6
John 10:10
John 15:11
Romans 3:23
Romans 5:8
Romans 6:23
Ephesians 1:7
1 John 1:5-9

Talk to your pastor if you have any questions about what it means to follow Christ. If you are not part of a local church, talk to a friend who is a follower of Christ.

You can always contact me via Facebook or e-mail me at **jasonmac@bellsouth.net**. I would love to hear from you.

My blog is located at **www.jasonmcnaughten.com**.

Also, please consider reviewing my book on **www.amazon.com**. Thanks!

Suggested Resources

Backus, William. *Healing Power of the Christian Mind, The: How Biblical Truth Can Keep You Healthy*. Minneapolis: Bethany House Publishers,   1998.

Backus, William, and Marie Chapian. *Telling Yourself the Truth: Find Your Way Out of Depression, Anxiety, Fear, Anger, and Other Common Problems by Applying the Principles of Misbelief Therapy*. 20th ed. Minneapolis: Bethany House Publishers, 2000.

Challem, Jack. *The Food-Mood Solution: All-Natural Ways to Banish Anxiety, Depression, Anger, Stress, Overeating, and Alcohol and Drug Problems--and Feel Good Again*. Hoboken, NJ: Wiley, 2008.

Hart, Archibald D., and Hart. *Adrenaline and Stress: the Exciting New Breakthrough That Helps You Overcome Stress Damage*. Revised ed. Dallas: Thomas Nelson Publishers, 1995.

----- *Unmasking Male Depression: Recognizing the Root Cause to Many Problem Behaviors Such as Anger, Resentment, Abusiveness, Silence, Addictions, and Sexual Compulsiveness*. Nashville: Thomas Nelson, 2001.

Ilardi, Stephen S. *The Depression Cure: the 6-Step Program to Beat Depression Without Drugs*. Reprint ed. Cambridge, MA: Da Capo Lifelong Books, 2010.

Iles, Curt. *The Mockingbird's Song*. Dry Creek, LA: Creekbank Stories, 2007.

Lloyd-Jones, David Martyn. *Spiritual Depression: Its Causes and Cure*. Grand Rapids, Mich.: Eerdmans Pub Co, 1965.

Minirth, Frank, and Paul Meier. *Happiness Is a Choice: the Symptoms, Causes, and Cures of Depression*. 2 ed. Grand Rapids, MI: Baker Books, 1994.

Newberry, Tommy. *The 4:8 Principle: the Secret to a Joy-Filled Life*. Carol Stream, IL: Tyndale House Publishers, Inc., 2007.

Porowski, James P., and Paul B. Carlisle. *Strength For the Journey: Biblical Perspective On Discouragement and Depression*. Nashville: LifeWay Christian Resources, 1999.

Scazzero, Peter. *The Emotionally Healthy Church: a Strategy for Discipleship That Actually Changes Lives*. Grand Rapids, MI: Zondervan, 2003.

Notes

[1]C. H. Spurgeon, *Lectures to My Students: Complete and Unabridged*, New ed. (Grand Rapids, MI: Zondervan, 1979), 154,160.

[2]*Diagnostic Criteria from Dsm-iv-tr* (Washington, D.C.: Amer Psychiatric Pub, 2000), 168.

[3]Archibald D. Hart, *Unmasking Male Depression: Recognizing the Root Cause of Many Problem Behaviors, Such as Anger, Resentment, Abusiveness, Silence, Addictions, and Sexual Compulsiveness* (Nashville: Thomas Nelson, 2001).

[4]Curt Iles, *The Mockingbird's Song* (Dry Creek, LA: Creekbank Stories, 2007), 168.

[5]Richard J. Krejcir, "Statistics On Pastors," Into Thy Word, http://www.intothyword.org/apps/articles/default.asp?articleid=36562&columnid=3958 (accessed October 3, 2013).

[6] Whitney, Donald S. "Psalms of the Day." Lecture, Midwestern Baptist Theological Seminary, Kansas City, MO, Fall, 2001.

[7] Stephen S. Ilardi, *The Depression Cure: the 6-Step Program to Beat Depression Without Drugs*, Reprint ed. (Cambridge, MA: Da Capo Lifelong Books, 2010), see chapter 4.

[8] Ilardi, 40.

[9] William Backus and Marie Chapian, *Telling Yourself the Truth: Find Your Way Out of Depression, Anxiety, Fear, Anger, and Other Common Problems by Applying the Principles of Misbelief Therapy*, 20th ed. (Minneapolis: Bethany House Publishers, 2000), 17.

[10] Maria Popiva, "A Simple Exercise to Increase Well-Being and Lower Depression from Martin Seligman, Founding Father of Positive Psychology," brain pickings, http://www.brainpickings.org/index.php/2014/02/18/martin-seligman-gratitude-visitthreeblessings/?utm_content=buffer4ae1d&utm_medium=social&utm_source=twitter.com&utm_ca mpaign=buffer?utm_source=facebook&utm_mediu m=social&utm_content=3982381 (accessed March 1, 2014).

[11] Peter Scazzero, *The Emotionally Healthy Church, Expanded Edition: a Strategy for Discipleship That Actually Changes Lives*, Exp ed. (Grand Rapids, MI: Zondervan, 2010), 166.

[12] "The Blessing of Unanswered Prayers (Unknown Confederate Soldier)," Christian Classics Ethereal Library,http://www.ccel.org/node/4529 (accessed February 4, 2014).

[13] Hara Estroff Marano, "Depression: A Family Matter," Psychology Today, http://www.psychologytoday.com/articles/200303/d epression-family-matter (accessed March 4, 2014).

[14] Paul W Powell, *Shepherding the Sheep in Smaller Churches* (Dallas: Annuity Board of the Southern Baptist Convention, 1995), 116.

[15] "On Mental Health Concerns and the Heart of God,"sbc.net, http://www.sbc. net/resolutions/am Resolution.asp?ID=1232 (accessed February 3, 2014).

Made in the USA
Columbia, SC
06 November 2019

82776540R00067